SLUGGERS' Car Wash

by Stuart J. Murphy • illustrated by Barney Saltzberg

HarperCollinsPublishers

MathStart® DOLLARS AND CENTS

LEVEL 3

To Annika—who is sure to become an entrepreneur
—S.J.M.

The publisher and author would like to thank teachers Patricia Chase, Phyllis Goldman, and
Patrick Hopfensperger for their help in making the math in MathStart just right for kids.

HarperCollins®, ☐®, and MathStart® are registered trademarks of HarperCollins Publishers.
For more information about the MathStart series, write to HarperCollins Children's Books,
1350 Avenue of the Americas, New York, NY 10019, or visit our website at www.mathstartbooks.com.

Bugs incorporated in the MathStart series design were painted by Jon Buller.

Library of Congress Cataloging-in-Publication Data
Murphy, Stuart J.
Sluggers' car wash / by Stuart J. Murphy
p.   cm. — (MathStart)
"Dollars and cents."
"Level 3."
Summary: When the 21st Street Sluggers, a baseball team, have a car wash to raise money, they
learn to keep careful track of their dollars and cents.
ISBN 0-06-028920-1 — ISBN 0-06-028921-X (lib. bdg.) — ISBN 0-06-446248-X (pbk.)
1. Addition—Juvenile literature.   2. Moneymaking projects for children—Juvenile literature
[1. Moneymaking projects—Fiction.   2. Car washes—Fiction.]   I. Title.   II. Series.
QA115 .M876 2001   00-054062
[E]—dc21

Typography by Elynn Cohen   1 2 3 4 5 6 7 8 9 10   ❖   First Edition

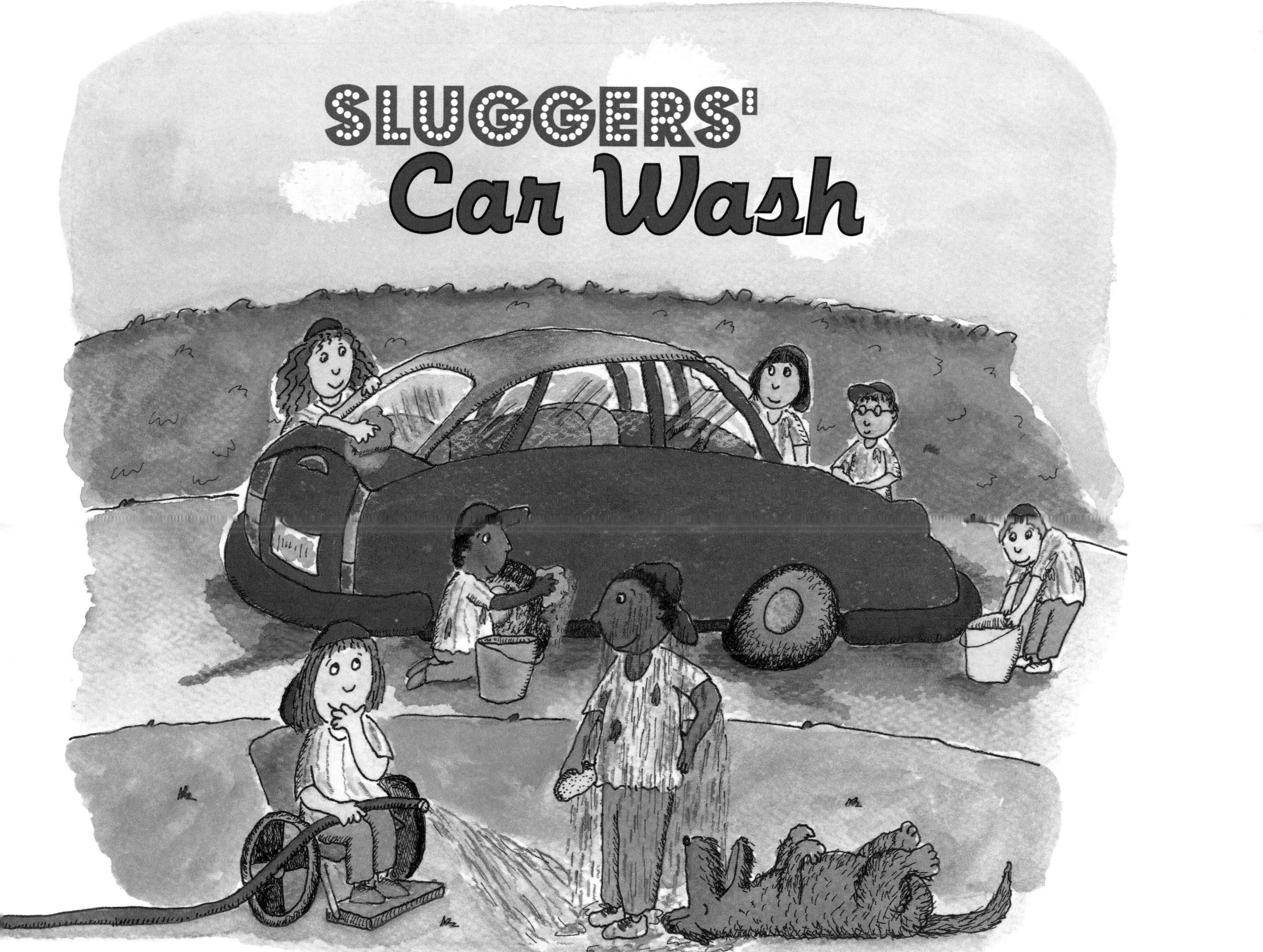
SLUGGERS'
Car Wash

The 21ˢᵗ Street Sluggers had a problem. They were going to be in the play-offs for the very first time.
That wasn't the problem.

In two weeks they had to play the 7th Avenue Spitfires.
That wasn't the problem either.

"Look at these T-shirts," said Julia. "They're worn-out, they're dirty, and they have holes the size of manhole covers. We've got to get some new T-shirts before the play-offs."

"That would cost a lot of money," said Lilly. "At least a hundred dollars."

"Coach said if we raised some money, he could probably get all the parents to match it," Julia reminded them.

"Yeah, but how are we going to raise money?" CJ demanded.
"I know!" said Will. "A car wash!"

8

"Hey, that's a great idea!" said Lilly. "We can get the whole team to help."

"All right!" said CJ. "Let's get started right away. We'll charge 3 dollars and 50 cents a car. Let's put all our money together. Then we can go out and buy supplies."

All the team members emptied their pockets. CJ kept a record of who gave what amount of money.

15 one-dollar bills: $15.00
20 quarters: $ 5.00
18 dimes: $ 1.80
24 nickels: $ 1.20
89 pennies: $ .89
                          $23.89

Then he sorted out the dollars and all the different coins. He made a decimal point between the dollars and the cents as he added everything up.

"We have 23 dollars and 89 cents," he announced. "That's almost 25 dollars."

"Lilly and Will, you guys go get soap and sponges," CJ directed. "Julia, you can get some poster board for signs."

"What are you going to do?" asked Julia as CJ handed out money to the Sluggers.

"I'm going to set up my office!" said CJ.

Before long everyone was back from their errands. They gave CJ the change.

Sponges: $8.13

Soap: $4.75

Poster board: $4.50

$17.38

CJ counted up the money they had left.
While Will made a big sign, CJ got a chair and
a beach umbrella. While Lilly filled the buckets
with water, CJ got himself a tall glass of lemonade.

2 one-dollar bills:	$2.00
7 quarters:	$1.75
8 dimes:	$ .80
24 nickels:	$1.20
76 pennies:	$ .76
	$6.51

They didn't have to wait very long. Will's mom was their first customer. Julia was in charge of the hose, Will had the soap, Lilly handed out sponges, and the Sluggers all started to wash.

Soon Will's mom drove her clean car over to the cash table.
She handed CJ a five-dollar bill.

"Let's see, 3 dollars and 50 cents plus two quarters makes 4 dollars, and a dollar bill makes 5 dollars," said CJ. He handed her 1 dollar and 50 cents. "Tell your friends to come to the Sluggers' Car Wash!"

Then he figured out how much money they had now.

"Keep working, guys!" he shouted. "We've got a long way to go!"

1 five-dollar bill:	$ 5.00
1 one-dollar bill:	$ 1.00
5 quarters:	$ 1.25
8 dimes:	$ .80
24 nickels:	$ 1.20
76 pennies:	$ .76
	$10.01

19

A red convertible was next.

Will scrubbed. Lilly polished. Julia squirted the hose. "Oops," she said.

The driver of the convertible handed CJ 2 one-dollar bills, 4 quarters, 4 dimes, and 2 nickels.

CJ counted. "Hmmm, 2 one-dollar bills plus 4 quarters makes 3 dollars, and 4 dimes is 40 cents, plus 2 nickels makes 50 cents. That's 3 dollars and 50 cents— exact change. We appreciate your business!" CJ said with a bow.

21

The Sluggers washed a green pickup. Julia squirted. Lilly polished. Will scrubbed. "Oops," he said.

CJ sipped his lemonade.

The driver gave CJ a ten-dollar bill. CJ counted. "Hmm, 3 dollars and 50 cents plus 2 quarters makes 4 dollars, plus 1 dollar makes 5 dollars, plus 5 dollars makes 10 dollars." He gave her back 6 dollars and 2 quarters.

Next was a yellow station wagon.
Will scrubbed. Julia squirted. Lilly slipped. "Yuck!" she said.

"Hurry it up, guys," yelled CJ. "There's a blue Jeep right behind you!"

The driver of the station wagon gave CJ a five-dollar bill and 2 quarters. "Just give me back 2 singles," he said.

"Okay, 3 dollars and 50 cents, 4 dollars and 50 cents, 5 dollars and 50 cents," said CJ as he handed over the 2 bills.

SLUGGERS
CAR
WASH
TODAY

When there was a break in traffic, CJ figured out on his clipboard how much money they had now.

Keep scrubbing, guys!

1 ten-dollar bill:	$10.00
1 five-dollar bill:	$ 5.00
9 quarters:	$ 2.25
12 dimes:	$ 1.20
26 nickels:	$ 1.30
76 pennies:	$ .76
	$20.51

"We're getting there!" CJ called out.
Cars came all afternoon.

Finally the last car was washed. CJ gave the Sluggers back all the money they'd chipped in to buy supplies and counted up what was left.

3 ten-dollar bills: $30.00
5 five-dollar bills: $25.00
6 one-dollar bills: $ 6.00
6 quarters: $ 1.50
1 dime: $ .10
9 nickels: $ .45
7 pennies: $ .07
                        $63.12

Team: $ 63.12
Parents: $ 63.12
          $126.24

"Wow," he said. "When our parents double that amount, we'll definitely have enough for new T-shirts! We did great!"

29

"Oh, we did, did we?" said Will.

"I guess so," said Lilly. "Most of us worked really hard. And most of us are really hot. And really tired. And really wet. But I notice one of us isn't."

"Well, I know how to fix that!" said Julia.

31

In *Sluggers' Car Wash* the math concept is counting dollars and cents. The ability to count money and to make change is a basic skill needed for everyday life.

If you would like to have more fun with the math concepts presented in *Sluggers' Car Wash*, here are a few suggestions:

- As you read the story, help the child understand what is happening on the clipboard. You might cover up the totals and ask questions like, "How much was spent on supplies?" or "How much did the children have after they washed Will's mom's car?"

- Help the child figure out how many cars would have to be washed to reach the Sluggers' goal of 100 dollars. (Remember that the Sluggers only have to make half of the 100 dollars themselves.) After rereading the story, help the child determine how many cars were actually washed.

- Have the child make a chart that shows how to make 1 dollar using like coins. The chart might look like this:

Pennies	Nickels	Dimes	Quarters	Half-Dollars	Dollars
100	20	10	4	2	1

Then explore ways to make 1 dollar by using combinations of different coins.

- Give child a number of 5- and 1-dollar bills and some coins. Have the child sort the money (all the pennies together, all the nickels together, etc.), write down the amounts, and then determine the total.

Following are some activities that will help you extend the concepts presented in *Sluggers' Car Wash* into a child's everyday life:

Shopping: Use a catalog or newspaper insert and have the child pretend that he or she is going shopping. Give the child 10 dollars either in real bills and coins or in play money. The child chooses items to "buy." After "buying" each item, he or she sets aside the money spent and counts up how much remains.

Eating Out: The next time you go out to eat, have the child pick what he or she wants from the menu and then calculate how much it will cost. Name a denomination higher than the meal's total and ask what the change would be.

Count the Difference: Take 20 index cards and write a different monetary value on each. Use both dollars and cents, but no card should be more than 3 dollars. Place the cards facedown in a pile. Create a "bank" of about 50 dollars in real or play money. The first player selects 2 cards, counts out the difference between the 2 amounts, and takes that amount out of the bank. (For example, a player who draws 2 cards worth $2.20 and $1.80, respectively, gets 40 cents.) When all the cards have been played, the player with the most money is the winner.

The following books include some of the concepts presented in *Sluggers' Car Wash*:

- ALEXANDER, WHO USED TO BE RICH LAST SUNDAY by Judith Viorst

- HOW THE SECOND GRADE GOT $8,205.50 TO VISIT THE STATUE OF LIBERTY by N. Zimelman

33